UNIVERSITY OF MINNESOTA

Carl Sandburg

BY GAY WILSON ALLEN

UNIVERSITY OF MINNESOTA PRESS • MINNEAPOLIS

Printed in the United States of America at
Jones Press, Minneapolis

Library of Congress Catalog Card Number: 72-619528
ISBN 0-8166-0644-7

The poem "Wistful" and lines from "Pencils" from *Smoke and Steel* by Carl Sandburg, copyright 1920 by Harcourt Brace Jovanovich, Inc.; copyright 1948 by Carl Sandburg. Reprinted by permission of the publishers. Lines from "To a Contemporary Bunkshooter," "Mamie," "The Shovel Man," and "Chicago" from *Chicago Poems* by Carl Sandburg. Copyright 1916 by Holt, Rinehart and Winston, Inc. Copyright 1944 by Carl Sandburg. Reprinted by permission of Harcourt Brace Jovanovich, Inc. Lines from "Prairie," "Handfuls," "Loam," "A Million Young Workmen, 1915," and "The Four Brothers" from *Cornhuskers* by Carl Sandburg. Copyright 1918 by Carl Sandburg. Copyright 1946 by Holt, Rinehart and Winston, Inc. Reprinted by permission of Holt, Rinehart and Winston, Inc.

PUBLISHED IN THE UNITED KINGDOM AND INDIA BY THE OXFORD UNIVERSITY PRESS, LONDON AND DELHI, AND IN CANADA BY THE COPP CLARK PUBLISHING CO. LIMITED, TORONTO

CARL SANDBURG

GAY WILSON ALLEN, a professor emeritus of English at New York University, is the author of a number of works of literary scholarship, including *The Solitary Singer: A Critical Biography of Walt Whitman, William James: A Biography, Herman Melville and His World*, and *A William James Reader*.

⤴ *Carl Sandburg*

CARL SANDBURG never won the Nobel Prize, but some Americans thought that he should have, and when Hemingway received it in 1954 he told reporters that it should have gone to Sandburg. Later in the year at the National Book Awards program in New York when Harvey Breit, of the *New York Times Book Review* staff, asked Sandburg how he felt about Hemingway's friendly gesture, he replied: "Harvey Breit, I want to tell you that sometime thirty years from now when the Breit boys are sitting around, one boy will say, 'Did Carl Sandburg ever win the Nobel Prize?' and one Breit boy will say, 'Ernest Hemingway gave it to him in 1954.'"

Whether or not Sandburg deserved the Nobel Prize, he was at least as well known and widely read in his own country as Hemingway, though perhaps not as famous abroad, for he had not outrun General Patton's tanks in the World War II invasion of Germany or led the vanguard in "liberating" Paris, to mention only two of Hemingway's fabulous adventures. Yet in his own way Sandburg was also newsworthy. No other American writer was at the same time so widely read and heard: hundreds of audiences had been entertained by his baritone voice, reading his poems, singing American folk ballads which he had collected, accompanying himself on his ubiquitous guitar, the familiar lock of unruly hair drooping over one eye. Innumerable photographs in newspapers and magazines and animated images on television and motion picture screens had made his face as much of a popular icon as Mark Twain's a generation earlier.

Of course these comparisons only establish the fact that Carl Sandburg was a great celebrity and a superb professional enter-

tainer. Was he a great poet? At the peak of his productivity — say
from 1930 to the entry of the United States in World War II —
there seemed little doubt that he was, though even then some
dissenting critical voices could be heard. By the time of his death
in the late 1960's his reputation seemed less secure, though as a
biographer of Lincoln he had no contemporary rival, and as a
symbolical "voice of America" he was rivaled only by the New
England poet Robert Frost, who bitterly resented any compari-
son. Actually, the competition of poets is always a mitigating
factor in their reputations, especially contemporary. Friends of
Frost tended to downgrade the prosodically freewheeling Sandburg. Admirers of T. S. Eliot were not inclined to hold a high
opinion of the folksy author of *The People, Yes.* Though Ezra
Pound had some appreciation of the revolutionary modernity of
Sandburg, he "put him down," as Ben Jonson did Shakespeare,
for his "small Latin and less Greek," or in Pound's own words,
as "a lumberjack who has taught himself all that he knows."
Lumberjacking happened to be one of the few occupations Sandburg had never tried, but he was unquestionably self-taught.

Whatever Carl Sandburg's future rank in literature may be —
and posthumous reputations are impossible to predict (witness
Melville, Whitman, and Emily Dickinson) — he was, as Thomas
Lask declared in the *New York Times* at the time of Sandburg's
death on July 23, 1967, "the American bard. The sense of being
American informed everything he wrote." Sandburg's success as
the voice and conscience of his time and generation, to a degree
Whitman would have envied, is sufficient justification for a critical study of his life and career. This is the most rewarding ap-
proach to this enormously productive writer. The question of his
"minor" or "major" status can wait for time to answer.

The America Sandburg knew and wrote about — at least until
after World War II — was "mid-America," life on the prairies of
Illinois and the shores of Lake Michigan from Milwaukee to

Chicago and Harbert, Michigan. His mind was still lively and his typewriter busy during most of his final twenty-two years at Flat Rock, North Carolina, but his formative years were spent in the Midwest of his contemporaries Theodore Dreiser, Sherwood Anderson, Sinclair Lewis, Edgar Lee Masters, and Ernest Hemingway — the Hemingway of the Nick Adams stories, which some critics think his best. It can hardly be accidental that these men who were some of the most innovative and influential authors in America from World War I to the beginning of World War II all had a similar background. By the end of World War II the spurt of midwestern literary energy had nearly spent itself and passed to the South. But the two decades between the wars were dominated by these mid-American poets and novelists.

In changing the course of American literature Sandburg and his western contemporaries were, to be sure, assisted by their equally western predecessors Mark Twain, Hamlin Garland, and William Dean Howells. All of these writers were largely self-taught, like Abraham Lincoln, who grew up in Indiana and Illinois. The first white settlers to arrive in this region in their covered wagons, like the later impoverished emigrants from northern Europe, had had little formal education, and the traditions they brought with them were severely tested and modified by the harsh life of the frontier and the crude towns built in reckless haste. Experience was their school. The world that Dreiser, Anderson, Sandburg, and Hemingway knew bore little resemblance to the cultured society of Henry James, Edith Wharton, and Edwin Arlington Robinson. Empiricism shaped both their ethics and their aesthetics. In this sense they were all "from Missouri," skeptical of authority, disdainful of conventions, and personally independent to the point of eccentricity. Consequently their attitude toward human experience was realistic, the subject of their fiction and verse the life of ordinary people, and their style shaped by the idiom and rhythms of mid-American speech.

These midwestern writers were acutely conscious of social inequalities and injustices, and several were professed Socialists, including Sandburg. In religion they were mainly agnostic, though tolerant of the religious experience of others, and they had a somewhat Emersonian attitude toward nature (Emerson was always one of Sandburg's favorite authors). Their life-style was stubbornly individualistic, in speech, manners, opinions, and artistic self-expression. Sandburg's clothes never seemed to fit properly, and his indifference to his appearance was so pronounced as finally to suggest a theatrical pose; but it was entirely in character with the role he played in lecturing and singing ballads, and in harmony, too, with his own personality, for clothes were never more than a practical necessity to him.

Sandburg's indifference to fashion began with his early life in Galesburg, Illinois, where he was born January 6, 1878, near the tracks of the Chicago, Burlington, and Quincy Railroad, for which his father worked as a blacksmith. Both parents were Swedish immigrants who had come to the United States separately. Clara Anderson was working as a hotel chambermaid in another small Illinois town when she met August Sandburg, member of a railroad gang passing through. They were married in 1874 and settled in Galesburg after August was transferred to the C.B.&Q. repair shop. He could read his Swedish Bible but never learned to write, having to sign his name with an X. Mrs. Sandburg could write personal letters in colloquial Swedish and phonetically spelled English. Neither was the least interested in books, except for the Bible, and Carl had to discover the world of literature without any encouragement at home.

In primary school Carl learned the alphabet and began reading in a "primer" which had puzzling sentences about a ladies' tea party. He had never tasted tea (the Swedes preferred coffee) and he thought the ladies' conversation very silly. But he soon became fascinated by words, spoken or written. Several years later he received a card from the public library and became an avid reader, especially of history and biographies of American Revolution heroes. He was disappointed to find the biographies of Civil War generals dull and unconvincing; strange, he thought, because he had talked with men who had fought in this more recent war and he found their stories absorbingly interesting. Many of the older people in Galesburg remembered Lincoln's debate with Judge Douglas at Knox College. A plaque on one of the buildings commemorated the historic spot, and Sandburg many times stopped to read it.

One of the subjects young Sandburg enjoyed most in school was geography; both the places and the people in other parts of the world stirred his imagination. Literature did not yet arouse much enthusiasm in him, especially the poetry of Longfellow and the novels of Dickens, his teachers' favorites. He read *Tom Sawyer* and *Huckleberry Finn,* but at the time preferred James Otis' *Toby Tyler: or, Ten Weeks with a Circus,* and Charles Coffin's *The Boys of '76.* He read detective stories, too, of course out of school, but found them less absorbing than Champlin's *Young Folks' Cyclopaedia of Persons and Places.* He was not bored by school, however, and liked most of his teachers, but after he finished the eighth grade he had to go to work to help his father support the family of five children (not counting two boys who died of diphtheria at an early age). But for a bright, observant, and gregarious boy with endless curiosity and a sympathetic nature, education really began after he quit school. In his own revealing account of his boyhood in *Always the Young Strangers* (1953) he could say, looking back from maturity:

"In those years as a boy in that prairie town I got education in scraps and pieces of many kinds, not knowing that they were part of my education. I met people in Galesburg who were puzzling to me, and later when I read Shakespeare I found those same people were puzzling him. I met little wonders of many kinds among animals and plants that never lost their wonder for me, and I found later that these same wonders had a deep interest for Emerson, Thoreau, and Walt Whitman. I met superstitions, folk tales, and folklore while I was a young spalpeen, 'a broth of a boy,' long before I read books about them. All had their part, small or large, in the education I got outside of books and schools."

Not surprisingly, it was also outside school that the "young spalpeen" learned "that crime and politics are tangled with each other, that law and justice sometimes can be a monkey business with a bad smell." He made this declaration in *Always the Young Strangers* regarding a particularly revolting murder in Chicago of a Dr. Cronin, "leader in a camp of the Clan-na-Gael fighters for the freedom of Ireland." One of the accused was "handy at passing money to jurymen" and went free. Another man allegedly connected with the murder "went free in a hurry on 'habeas corpus,' later was put on trial for jury bribing, and wriggled out free."

"Of course," Sandburg continues, "we got education out of the Cronin murder and the first and second trials. We learned that in time of peace, and no war on, men can kill a man not for money but because the man stands for something they hate and they want him out of the way. We learned that juries can be fixed, that if a convicted man waits a few years and gets a second trial there may be important witnesses who have died or moved away or somehow can't be found. . . . We learned things we didn't hear about in the Seventh Ward school and we never read about them in the detective stories of those days. . . ."

After a great variety of short-term jobs, delivering milk, cutting ice on the lake, assisting carpenters, painters, plumbers, barbers, druggists, etc., Sandburg decided at eighteen to see the country by traveling as a hobo to the wheat fields of Kansas. He rode freight trains, stopping at towns along the way to earn a little money at dishwashing or other temporary employment. He met other hoboes and shared food with them in their "jungles" near the railroad tracks. After working with a threshing crew he "bummed" his way to the Rocky Mountains and back home.

Sandburg was trying to learn the house-painting trade when the American battleship *Maine* was sunk in Havana harbor on February 15, 1898. Believing with most other Americans that Spain was responsible (exactly who or what caused the explosion has never been definitely known), he enlisted in the Sixth Infantry Regiment of the Illinois Volunteers. With this regiment he drilled for two months in Virginia, saw the national capitol while on leave, was transported to Guantánamo Bay in Cuba, then hastily shipped to Guánica, Puerto Rico, because of an epidemic of yellow fever in Cuba. The short war was nearly over before the Illinois soldiers arrived, and they saw no fighting, though they suffered in the tropical heat from wearing heavy wool Civil War uniforms, from thousands of insect bites, from dysentery and spoiled food which war profiteers had sold to the United States government.

As a "war veteran" Sandburg was admitted to Lombard College — the "other" college in Galesburg — without a high school diploma or an entrance examination. He supported himself by serving with the local fire department, studying and sleeping at night in the firehouse. The most remarkable teacher at Lombard, a man who won distinction later as an economist in Washington, D.C., was Professor Philip Green Wright. He taught English, mathematics, astronomy, and economics — some indication of the kind of college Lombard was. He took a special interest in Carl and gave him his first competent instruction in writing.

In college Sandburg played basketball and baseball, acted in a musical comedy, contributed to a literary magazine, and edited the college yearbook, but left in the spring of his senior year without a degree — probably because he had failed to take some

11

courses required for graduation. These courses may have been in mathematics, because this was one of the subjects which later prevented his passing the entrance examination to West Point after he had been nominated by his congressman. His other failure was in English grammar.

Though Sandburg left college without a definite goal in life, he had experienced the satisfaction of writing down his own thoughts and seeing them in print in the college publications. But he was restless and began wandering again, this time in the East. He spent ten days in a Pittsburgh jail (for "deadbeating" his way on a freight train) before returning to Galesburg. Home again and without employment, he completed a batch of poems. Professor Wright had a small printing press in his basement, and there Sandburg's first three slender volumes were set up and privately printed: *In Reckless Ecstasy* in 1904 and *The Plaint of a Rose* and *Incidentals* in 1905.

It might surprise readers of Sandburg's *Chicago Poems* to find that he derived the title of his first book from the popular, romantic, and third-rate contemporary Marie Corelli, who praised the "reckless ecstasies of language." At this stage in his development as a poet Sandburg believed simply that "there are depths of life that logic cannot sound. It takes feeling." To produce this *feeling* he used the galloping meter of a Kipling, or almost any other popular poet of the period, as in the embarrassingly trite "Pulse-Beats and Pen-Strokes":

> For the hovels shall pass and the shackles drop,
>   The gods shall tumble and the systems fall;
> And the things they will make, with their loves at stake,
>   Shall be the gladness of each and all.

However, *Incidentals,* a collection of aphorisms, was in a prose-poetry form suggestive of Sandburg's maturer style:

> What is shame?
> Shame is the feeling you have when you agree

> with the woman who loves you that you are the
> man she thinks you are . . .
>
> Truth consists of paradoxes and a paradox
> is two facts that stand on opposite hilltops
> and across the intervening valley call
> each other liars.

These juvenilia Sandburg was glad to forget, and they have never been reprinted, except for brief quotations in Harry Golden's *Carl Sandburg* and in an article I wrote for an academic magazine.

Chicago was the place that Sandburg later made famous in his poems, but he could have written a book on Galesburg, Illinois, similar to Sherwood Anderson's psychological study of people in *Winesburg, Ohio*, or epitaphs of tragic failure like those in Edgar Lee Masters' *Spoon River Anthology*. In fact, sketches of such stories and biographies Sandburg did publish in *Always the Young Strangers*, with the difference that the outright failures he mentions were few. Collectively the subjects of his sketches were a cross section of the nation, or in Sandburg's own words: "This small town of Galesburg, as I look back on it, was a piece of the American Republic. Breeds and blood strains that figure in history were there for me, as a boy to see and hear in their faces and their ways of talking and acting."

From 1902 to 1906 Sandburg wandered away and returned to Galesburg, supporting himself mainly by peddling stereoptican pictures, but he also contributed to a Chicago magazine called *Tomorrow*. In 1906 he became associate editor of another magazine in Chicago called *Lyceumite*, and began giving lectures on Walt Whitman. It was in Chicago that he met Winfield R. Gaylord, an organizer of the Social Democratic party in Wisconsin. The doctrines of the party strongly appealed to him and he accepted an offer to join Mr. Gaylord in his work.

Sandburg continued to lecture on Whitman, but gave most of

his time to traveling and addressing workingmen in Wisconsin. "Labor is beginning to realize its power," he told them. "We no longer beg, we demand old-age pensions; we demand a minimum wage; we demand industrial accident insurance; we demand unemployment insurance; and we demand the eight-hour day, which must become the basic law of the land." These demands which seemed so radical in 1907–9 would become "the basic law of the land," not under a Socialist president but under the administration of Franklin D. Roosevelt and be extended in subsequent Democratic and Republican administrations. Yet the pioneers for these laws were those Wisconsin Socialists La Follette and Gaylord, and party recruiters like Carl Sandburg.

One day in 1908 at the Milwaukee Socialist headquarters Sandburg met Lilian Steichen, a schoolteacher from Illinois, who was there because she had been employed by the party to translate Socialist classics from French and German into English. She and Sandburg were immediately attracted to each other and were married several months later, a happy marriage that lasted until Sandburg's death. Mrs. Sandburg was the sister of Edward Steichen, who became a world-famous photographer and one of the poet's staunchest friends.

From recruiting members for the Socialist party Sandburg made an easy transition to Milwaukee journalism. He did reporting and wrote feature articles and some editorials for the *News*, the *Sentinel*, and the *Journal*. Milwaukee elected a Socialist mayor, Emil Seidel, and he employed Sandburg as a private secretary. But newspaper work remained his chief vocation. In 1912 he joined the liberal *Milwaukee Leader*, then went to the *Chicago Daily World* and, several newspaper jobs later, to the *Chicago Daily News*, with which he remained until the success of his biography of Lincoln, *The Prairie Years*, made it possible for him to resign and buy a farm in Harbert, Michigan, where his wife raised goats and he could give his full time to poetry and biography, with intervals of lecturing.

Sandburg's fierce sympathy with poor people, the oppressed and the exploited, which was to find expression in all his writing — in fact, was often the main reason for his writing at all — became permanently imbedded in his conscience and consciousness during his few years of propagating socialism in Wisconsin. However, he was never a Marxist, though he had read *Das Kapital* at Lombard with Professor Wright. He was more of a Populist and social reformer, perhaps influenced somewhat by "Teddy" Roosevelt in the early years of the twentieth century, and certainly by the muckraking journalists: Ida Tarbell, who wrote about the greed of John D. Rockefeller; Lincoln Steffens, who uncovered political corruption in the cities; and Upton Sinclair, the Socialist novelist, who shocked the nation into beginning pure-food legislation after *The Jungle* (1906) revealed the incredibly unsanitary conditions of the packing industry in Chicago. (Sinclair's equally strong indictment of the exploitation of laboring men, especially the nearly illiterate newcomers from Europe, by factory employers, real-estate dealers, and merchants did not produce such prompt results.) Sandburg, like Sinclair, was more concerned with the actual condition of the workingmen's lives than with ideology.

In 1908 Sandburg campaigned for Eugene V. Debs for the presidency, and in 1915 he and Jack London often wrote the entire contents of the *International Socialist Review*, using a variety of pseudonyms. At the outbreak of World War I he shared the pacifist views of other Socialists (Social Democrats in Wisconsin, trade-union Socialists in New York City, Fabians in England, and Christian Socialists in Germany, France, and Italy). He expressed his horror of killing in a group of "War Poems" (1914–15), and in the *International Socialist Review* he argued that soldiers were actually exploited laborers:

"It's a workingman's world. Shovels and shovelling take more time of soldiers than guns and shooting. Twenty-one million men on the battlefields of Europe are shovelling more than shooting. Not only have they dug hundreds of miles of trenches, but around and under the trenches are tunnels and labyrinthian catacombs. All dug by shovels. Technically, in social science and economics, the soldier is a parasite and a curious louse of the master-class imposed on the working class. Yet strictly now the soldier is a worker, a toiler on and under the land. He's a sucker, a shovel-man who gets board and clothes from the government that called him to the colors. A mucker-gun-man — that's what a soldier is."

Yet when the United States finally entered World War I, Sandburg broke with the Social Democrats and supported President Wilson. As Harry Golden recalls, "Outside Milwaukee the Wisconsin Socialists never made great headway until 1918, when they got the votes of many people of German descent who opposed America's entry into World War I. It was the kind of success that helped kill [the party]."

Sandburg never returned to the Socialist party, but he remained personally loyal to Debs and invited him to his home in suburban Chicago after Debs was released from prison. In 1933 Sandburg lost the friendship of Robert Frost by supporting Roosevelt and the New Deal. Six years later President Roosevelt warmly thanked him for a radio broadcast endorsing his policies and candidacy for a second term. Sandburg also did some campaigning for John F. Kennedy in 1960. He could count Justice William O. Douglas and Adlai Stevenson as personal friends, but at the same time he admired Republican Earl Warren. Thus the Social Democrat of the early twentieth century was, by mid-century, securely in the mainstream of American politics.

While still extremely busy in newspaper work and writing articles and editorials for Socialist magazines, Sandburg somehow found time to compose the poems which began to create a literary reputation for him when *Chicago Poems* was published in 1916. Some of these poems had attracted attention when first published by Harriet Monroe in *Poetry*, a magazine she started in Chicago in 1912. In fact, his poetic fame might be said to have begun with the publication of "Chicago" in *Poetry* in 1914. This was the key poem in the collection Henry Holt and Company published, a volume declared by Amy Lowell in the *New York Times Book Review*, to be "one of the most original books this age has produced."

In "Chicago" Sandburg admits all the faults of the city familiar to the world as the "stormy, husky, brawling . . . crooked . . . brutal" place where painted women lure farm boys under the gas lamps, gunmen kill and go free to kill again, and factory workers and their families starve because of low wages or unemployment. But this is not a social-protest poem. It is a lyric tribute to the vibrant, proud, happy, and laughing "City of the Big Shoulders . . . a tall bold slugger set vivid against the little soft cities . . ." If Chicago lacks the culture and beauty of the older cities, its inhabitants can take pride in its youth, vitality, and joy in being alive. This is the Chicago myth created by Sandburg, and it gave a great stimulation to midwestern literature.

In "Skyscraper" the poet strives to give the building a "soul." The skyscraper, he says, acquired its soul from the men who built it, those who dug the foundation, erected the girders, carried the mortar, laid the brick and fitted the stone, strung miles of wires and pipes; and later the stenographers, scrubbing women, and watchmen who worked in it. He ignores the business executives, but perhaps they have no soul-power to spare. Anyway, this is the manner in which the poet humanizes inanimate steel and stone.

In his newspaper prose Sandburg continued to fight for the causes he had espoused since his first affiliation with the Social Democratic party, but in most of his poems he attacked social evils obliquely. One exception was "To a Contemporary Bunk Shooter" (previously printed in *New Masses* undisguised as "Billy Sunday"):

> You come along . . . tearing your shirt. . . . yelling about Jesus.
>
> . . . .
>
> He never came near clean people or dirty people but they felt cleaner because he came along. It was your crowd of bankers and business men and lawyers hired the sluggers and murderers who put Jesus out of the running.

He calls Billy Sunday "a bug-house peddler of second-hand gospel," telling "people living in shanties" that they can live in "mansions in the skies after they're dead and the worms have eaten 'em." Doubtless Billy Sunday deserved this cuffing, but the poem was indeed propaganda for the *New Masses*.

A prominent theme in *Chicago Poems* is the longing of ordinary people for the beauty and happiness they have never known. This clutching at dreams was not a creation of Sandburg's fantasy, but a social phenomenon which he accurately observed. The fact is confirmed by the contemporary midwestern novelists, Dreiser especially, whose early novels are repositories of social history. For example, in *Sister Carrie* (1900) the heroine is an unsophisticated girl who leaves a small town in Wisconsin to go to Chicago in search of pleasure and excitement. She finds only poverty, drudgery, and monotony until, by instinctive self-preservation from cold and hunger, she becomes a "kept woman." Yet in spite of subsequent fame and wealth in the theater, she never finds self-fulfillment, and continues dreaming of the happiness she has somehow missed. Many of the people in Sandburg's poems are brothers and sisters of Sister Carrie, such as "Mamie":

> Mamie beat her head against the bars of a little Indiana town and dreamed of romance and big things off somewhere the way the railroad trains all ran.

She thought of suicide and then decided that, "if she was going to die she might as well die struggling for a clutch of romance among the streets of Chicago."

> She has a job now at six dollars a week in the basement of the Boston store
> And even now she beats her head against the bars in the same old way and wonders if there is a bigger place the railroads run to from Chicago where maybe there is
>> romance
>> and big things
>> and real dreams
>> that never go smash.

A more cheerful theme in *Chicago Poems* is the laughter and joy workmen manage to find in spite of their toil and poverty. The face of the Jewish fish crier on Maxwell Street is the face "of a man terribly glad to be selling fish, terribly glad that God made fish, and customers to whom he may call his wares from a pushcart." The poet searches for "Happiness" and finds it one Sunday afternoon on the banks of the Desplaines River in "a crowd of Hungarians under the trees with their women and children and a keg of beer and an accordion." In "Fellow Citizens" the poet is told by a millionaire, an advertising executive named Jim Kirch, and the mayor that they are happy, but he discovers a man on Gilpin Place, near Hull House, making accordions and guitars which he plays himself after he has finished them, and "he had it all over the butter millionaire, Jim Kirch and the mayor when it came to happiness."

In the use of slang and undignified language Sandburg achieved in actuality the theory which Wordsworth set forth in his Preface to *Lyrical Ballads*: to "present incidents and situations from common life . . . in a selection of language really used by men . . ." Sandburg's poems are also more realistic than Wordsworth's, or even naturalistic (in the Zola sense), as in "The Walking Man of Rodin," with "The skull found always crumbling neighbor of the ankles." Yet Sandburg is also just as definitely romantic in his ability to see beauty in the commonplace. "The Shovel Man," for example, is

> A dago working for a dollar six bits a day
> And a dark-eyed woman in the old country dreams of him
> for one of the world's ready men with a pair of fresh lips
> and a kiss better than all the wild grapes that ever grew
> in Tuscany.

Perhaps it is not surprising that Sandburg most often found this beauty in the lives of foreign-born workmen, people like his own Swedish parents; but these recent Americans also constituted a large segment of the Chicago population. Sandburg was indeed at this period the Chicago poet.

In his second volume of poetry, *Cornhuskers* (1918), Sandburg played less the role of the urban poet and wrote more about rural sights and sounds and his wider experiences during World War I. He was now traveling more, lecturing, reading his poems, collecting and singing the folk ballads which he published later in *The American Songbag* (1927). His three daughters (Margaret, born in 1911, Janet in 1914, and Helga in 1918) also began to have an emotional effect on his literary imagination as he entertained them with the kind of child-fantasy stories he published in 1922 in *Rootabaga Stories*.

Cornhuskers opens with "Prairie," a poem partly autobiographical, partly cosmic, partly prophetic:

> I was born on the prairie and the milk of its wheat, the red
> of its clover, the eyes of its women, gave me a song and a
> slogan.

> Here the water went down, the icebergs slid with gravel, the
> gaps and the valleys hissed, and the black loam came, and
> the yellow sandy loam.

> ᵒ ·

O prairie mother, I am one of your boys.

. . . .

I speak of new cities and new people.
I tell you the past is a bucket of ashes.
I tell you yesterday is a wind gone down,
    a sun dropped in the west.
I tell you there is nothing in the world,
    only an ocean of tomorrows,
    a sky of tomorrows.

I am a brother of the cornhuskers who say
    at sundown:
            Tomorrow is a day.

In these poems Sandburg shows his fondness for elemental things: sky, moon, stars, wind, birds, and animals. He celebrates nature in all seasons, but especially late summer and autumn: the ripening corn, the yellow cornflower in autumn wind, the blue of larkspur and Canadian thistle, and red-ripe tomatoes. In "Wilderness" he feels kinship with a wolf, a fox, a hog, a fish, a baboon, an eagle, and a mockingbird, and exclaims, "O, I got a zoo, I got a menagerie, inside my ribs." But he is over-fond of baby metaphors. In "Baby Face" the "white moon comes in on a baby face." In "The Year" buds "open baby fists / Into hands of broad flowers," while the winds sing "lullabies." "Handfuls" narrowly escapes sentimentality:

> Blossoms of babies
> Blinking their stories
> Come soft
> On the dusk and the babble;
> Little red gamblers,
> Handfuls that slept in the dust.

This book is dedicated to Janet and Margaret, each of whom gets a poem. In "Sixteen Months" the adoring father sees on Janet's lips the blue mist of dreams, smoke, and haze on "ten miles of corn" in morning sunlight. This is stretching metaphors to their limit. As "Child Margaret" writes the Arabic symbols, 1 and 7 have a military stance, 6 and 9 dance, 2 is a trapeze actor, 3 is humpbacked, and 8 knock-kneed. "Each number is a bran-new rag doll." This whimsical side of the poet may have surprised some readers who had Sandburg tagged as "the Chicago poet."

But Sandburg was a poet of many moods. In "Sunset from Omaha Hotel Window" he finds "The gloaming is bitter / As in Chicago / or Kenosha." From the observation car of a train he enjoys the "Still Life" pictures of the rolling prairie, new-mown hay, Holstein cows, a signalman in a Kansas City tower. Sitting by a steam radiator on a winter day he thinks about "Horses and Men in Rain," delivering milk or coal, grocery boys, mail carriers. His memory and sympathy are panoramic, like Whitman's in "Song of Myself"; but also nostalgic, and his empathy is selective, not the all-embracing compassion of the Messianic Whitman. He empathizes with the Greeks he saw in Keokuk working on a railroad; a pawnshop operator on a back street; lonely men in oyster boats in the Chesapeake Bay. He writes elegies for Adelaide Crapsey, the Brooklyn girl who composed poems in Japanese forms while dying of an incurable illness; for Don Magregor, the Colorado miner accused of murder, who died with Pancho Villa in Mexico; Buffalo Bill, hero of prairie boys; and "Old Osawatomie," now "six feet of dust under the morning stars."

Sandburg has often been compared to Whitman, and he frequently wrote on the same themes, but always with his own handling of them. The long verses of "Prairie" look superficially like Whitman's form, but the music is different. A major distinction is in their treatment of the theme of death. To Whitman death was always beautiful, an old mother crooning a lullaby from the ocean of immortality, but to Sandburg death is the final irony of life — stillness, nothingness. In "Cool Tombs" Abraham Lincoln and his assassin, Ulysses Grant and the "con men" who brought shame to his administration, lovely Pocahontas and "a streetful of people" are all equalized "in the dust . . . in the cool tombs." This is one of Sandburg's most beautiful lyrics, and most devastatingly ironic. In "Grass" the scars of World War I will be covered by the perennial grass, not in a Pantheistic transmutation of men into vegetation, but as nature erases the scars of human violation of life. Instead of Whitman's consolation, one is reminded of Hemingway's *nada* — "it was all nada." In Shenandoah Valley lie "The blue nobody remembers, the gray nobody remembers . . ." But generalizing about the brevity of life and the sureness of death in "Loam" the poet does seem to find some consolation in the eternal cycle:

> In the loam we sleep,
>
> . . . .
>
>   We rise;
> To shape of rose leaf,
> Of face and shoulder.
>
>   We stand, then,
>   To a whiff of life,
> Lifted to the silver of the sun
> Over and out of the loam
>   A day.

And "In Tall Grass," seeing a honeycomb and bees buzzing "in the dried head of a horse in a pasture corner," he would "ask no better a winding sheet . . ."

Sandburg's first reaction to World War I was that of most Socialists throughout the world. In "A Million Young Workmen, 1915" he exclaims with the bitterness of Stephen Crane in *War Is Kind*:

> And oh, it would have been a great job of killing and a new and beautiful thing under the sun if the million knew why they hacked and tore each other to death.
>
> . . . .

I dreamed a million ghosts of the young workmen rose in
    their shirts all soaked in crimson . . . and yelled:
God damn the grinning kings, God damn the kaiser and the
    czar.

However, in "The Four Brothers," subtitled "Notes for War
Songs (November, 1917)," Sandburg's mood is that of Whitman
in his recruiting "Beat! Beat! Drums!":

I say now, by God, only fighters today will save the world,
    nothing but fighters will keep alive the names of those
    who left red prints of bleeding feet at Valley Forge in
    Christmas snow.

In fact, this is Sandburg's "Battle Hymn of the Republic," in
which he has an apocalyptic vision that

Out of it all a God who knows is sweeping clean,
Out of it all a God who sees and pierces through,
    is breaking and cleaning out an old thousand years,
    is making ready for a new thousand years.

In spite of its unevenness *Cornhuskers* is one of his finest
volumes of poems. The unevenness probably reflects the turbu-
lence of the period in which these poems were written, 1915–18.

Smoke and Steel (1920) also shows the excitement of the war
period, and some of the disillusionment of the aftermath, but
especially the former in the jazzy rhythms of "Honky Tonk in
Cleveland, Ohio" and "Jazz Fantasia." The title of the book is
misleading, for most of the poems are neither social protest nor
depiction of industrial life. In the title poem the poet sees
"smoke" not as pollution or factory ugliness but as a parallel to
human blood:

And always dark in the heart and through it,
    Smoke and the blood of a man.
Pittsburgh, Youngstown, Gary — they make their steel with men.

The last clause is not uttered in sarcasm, for the poet who had
prayed in *Cornhuskers* to be beaten on an anvil into a crowbar

or a rivet for a skyscraper saw inspiring strength and beauty in steel. In the blast furnaces he now sees "women dancing, / Dancing out of the flues and smokestacks . . ."

"The Sins of Kalamazoo," says Sandburg, are "neither scarlet nor crimson" but "a convict gray, a dishwater drab," and so is the place itself. Yet he has "loved the white dawn frost of early winter silver / And purple over your railroad tracks and lumber yards." Sandburg, one should remember, was a contemporary of the Ash Can School of painters, whom he had almost parodied in "Nocturne in a Deserted Brickyard" in *Chicago Poems*.

There are intimations, almost premonitions, of Eliot's *Waste Land* and "Hollow Men" in some passages in *Smoke and Steel*. In "Four Preludes on Playthings of the Wind" the cedar doors are broken and the golden girls vanished from the city which thought itself "the greatest city, / the greatest nation: / nothing like us ever was." Now the black crows caw and the rats scribble their hieroglyphic footprints on dusty doorsills. The squabbling of European nations at the peace table had disillusioned Sandburg as early as March 1919, the date he gave for "The Liars":

> Across their tables they fixed it up,
> Behind their doors away from the mob.
> And the guns did a job that nicked off millions.
>
> .   .   .   .
>
> And now
> Out of the butcher's job
> And the boneyard junk the maggots have cleaned,
> Where the jaws of skulls tell the jokes of war ghosts,
> Out of this they are calling now: Let's go back where we were.
>
> .   .   .   .
>
> So I hear The People tell each other:
>
> .   .   .   .
>
> To hell with 'em all,
> The liars who lie to nations,
> The liars who lie to The People.

The closest Sandburg himself got to the war was as a Scripps newspaper correspondent in Stockholm from October 1918 to May 1919. His assignment was not the war itself but interviews with people who had been in or near the war zone, or had escaped the turmoil in Russia. His dispatches were little more than human-interest stories for newspaper readers. But crossing the North Atlantic in late autumn provoked atavistic sensations in the descendant of that ancient seafaring nation. However, seeing the many statues of kings on the streets of Stockholm aroused his democratic antipathy. He admired the Riksdag bridge held up by massive stones, and took special interest, as he would have in Chicago, in the old women selling apples or cleaning windows, and fishermen casting their nets beneath the bridge. So he decided that he would rather have young men read "five lines of one of my poems" than have a bronze statue on the "king's street."

An important influence unconnected with the war which became obvious in *Smoke and Steel* was the Japanese haiku. Sandburg had already become more aware of images because of the Imagistic movement discussed and practiced by Ezra Pound and Amy Lowell in Harriet Monroe's *Poetry*. However, though his "Fog" in *Chicago Poems* has often been cited as an Imagistic poem, it seems to have been written without any influence from Pound or Lowell. But the haiku taught him to insinuate cryptic wisdom in an image. In the folksy "Put Off the Wedding Five Times and Nobody Comes to It" he throws off the remark, "It will always come back to me in the blur of that hokku: The heart of a woman of thirty is like the red ball of the sun seen through a mist." ("Blur" seems inaccurate here; perhaps he means ambiguity.) A final section of short poems in *Smoke and Steel* contains several excellent adaptations of the Japanese haiku. For example, "Thin Strips":

Under a peach tree I saw petals scattered
. . . torn strips of a bride's dress. I heard
a woman laugh many years ago.

Or "Wistful":

Wishes left on your lips
The mark of their wings.
Regrets fly kites in your eyes.

Sandburg's third volume of poetry was followed not by another book of poems but by *Rootabaga Stories* (1922), stories he had made up to amuse his three little daughters. These stories have a fairy-tale sense of unreality, with transformations, actions that defy gravity, and the reduction of winds, moons, landscapes, and human actions to child-fantasy dimensions. But much of the fun is in the names and places, with their absurd sounds, outrageous puns, and comic imagery. There is the family that named its first boy Gimme the Ax and its first girl Ax Me No Questions. Jason Squiff wears a popcorn hat, popcorn mittens, and popcorn shoes. Henry Hagglyhoagly plays the guitar with his mittens on. Another story tells how "The animals lost their tails and got them back again traveling from Philadelphia to Medicine Hat." These are not Aesop fables or miraculous stories with a moral. The "morals" are themselves jokes, like "Never Kick a Slipper at the Moon" when the moon looks like the toe and heel of a dancer's foot, for the shoe will go on to the moon. The verbal humor is the strongest indication that these tales were written by a poet.

The year following the publication of *Rootabaga Stories* Sandburg discussed with Alfred Harcourt, a New York publisher then working for Henry Holt, what book to write next. He had been interested in Abraham Lincoln since his boyhood, and for some years had been collecting Lincoln material: books, newspaper clippings, anecdotes told by people he met, and subjective impressions. Mindful of the success of Sandburg's book of stories for children, Harcourt suggested a life of Lincoln for teen-agers, and this was the book Sandburg intended to write when he began his first Lincoln biography. But the work grew in the writing until it became two hefty volumes, written in simple language, imaginative detail, and a fictional style acceptable in a juvenile book, but much too long and detailed for this genre. It was published as *Abraham Lincoln: The Prairie Years* (1926) for general readers.

The narrative of *Prairie Years* rests on the known facts of Lincoln's early life, but many basic facts were unknown, or had been blurred in oral transmission, or had become displaced by folklore. Thus Sandburg attempts to fill in missing information or to elaborate meager facts. Regarding Lincoln's legitimacy, he tells the rumors and mentions the ambiguities. He has no doubt that Lincoln himself was legitimate, but his grandmother, Lucy Hanks, was as a girl "too free and easy in her behavior," and had borne a child, Nancy, while living with a man she had not legally married. "What was clear in the years that had passed was that Lucy . . . had married a man she wanted, Henry Sparrow, and nine children had come and they were all learning to read and write under her teaching. Since she had married the talk about her running wild had let down."

Sandburg gives Nancy Hanks a husband, Thomas Lincoln, and imagines her home in May 1808, the year preceding Abraham Lincoln's birth:

"The Lincolns had a cabin of their own to live in. It stood among wild crab-apple trees.

"And the smell of wild crab-apple blossoms, and the low crying of all wild things, came keen that summer to the nostrils of Nancy Hanks.

"The summer stars that year shook out pain and warning, strange laughters, for Nancy Hanks."

The crabapple blossoms may well have been real, but how did the biographer know that "summer stars that year shook out pain and warning" to Nancy Hanks, as an annunciation of her future son of historic destiny? At the age of seven this son, himself, experiences spells of deep wonder, loneliness, and mysterious premonitions in the Indiana wilderness. His heroic qualities also soon begin to manifest themselves. At eighteen he can "take an ax at the end of the handle and hold it out in a straight horizontal line, easy and steady . . ." One day he walks thirty-four miles just to hear a lawyer make a speech. He becomes a famous wrestler, seemingly invincible. But he never misuses his fabulous strength, and of course his mind and character acquire the toughness and resilience, as if by supernatural design, which he will later need as president of a nation divided by a tragic war. He is the Cinderella hero of folklore, epic, and romance. And yet, in view of the incredible courage, strength, and endurance which Lincoln, as historical fact, did exhibit in the presidency, these symbolical details do not seem exaggerated, but possible and convincing.

Edmund Wilson has bitterly denounced Sandburg's biography of Lincoln (without distinguishing the *Prairie Years* from the *War Years*) as "romantic and sentimental rubbish." In *Patriotic Gore* he says, "there are moments when one is tempted to feel that the cruellest thing that has happened to Lincoln since he was shot by Booth has been to fall into the hands of Carl Sandburg." As an example, Wilson cites Sandburg's handling of the Ann Rutledge "love story":

"After the first evening in which Lincoln had sat next to her and found that bashful words tumbling from his tongue's end really spelled themselves out into sensible talk, her face, as he went away, kept coming back. So often all else would fade out of his mind and there would be only this riddle of a pink-fair face, a mouth and eyes in a frame of light corn-silk hair. He could ask himself what it meant and search his heart for an answer and no answer would come. A trembling took his body and dark waves ran through him sometimes when she spoke so simple a thing as, 'The corn is getting high, isn't it?' "

"The corn is getting high, indeed!" says Wilson. But he fails to give Sandburg credit for honestly admitting later that he had been "taken in" by this legend. When he condensed *The Prairie Years* for his one-volume *Abraham Lincoln* (1954) he changed the famous love affair to hypothesis and left out the "corny" description of Lincoln's emotions: "She was 21 and Lincoln 25 and in the few visits he had time for in this year when surveying and politics pressed him hard, he may have gone no further than to be a comforter. He may have touched and stroked her auburn hair once or more as he looked deep into her blue eyes and said no slightest word as to what hopes lay deep in his heart. . . . They were both young, with hope endless, and it could have been he had moments when the sky was to him a sheaf of blue dreams . . ."

As Lincoln grows up in *The Prairie Years* Sandburg has more historical documents to draw upon, and the Lincoln in the state legislature, in Congress, and in the Chicago convention which nominated him for the presidency is almost wholly believable. Of course for the Lincoln-Douglas debates there were the printed speeches themselves, and newspaper accounts of the campaign for the presidency. Though Sandburg consistently keeps his hero a man basically honest in spite of his driving ambition, he is shown making deals (or consenting to them after they are made by his supporters), compromising as any politician must, and following expediency rather than conscience when that is advantageous. Sandburg is especially effective in showing how circumstances often guided Lincoln's conduct. As the president-elect sets out for Washington to be inaugurated, he is still growing in stature, and in tragic foreboding, a hero in an epic which will end, as he himself half-suspects, in his own physical destruction.

The enormous financial success of *The Prairie Years* encouraged Sandburg to continue his biography through Lincoln's presidency. He now felt a heavy responsibility to tell the story completely and accurately, and he sought professional help from librarians, historians, and book dealers in assembling source material. For the first time in his life he had financial security, and he could concentrate on his one consuming ambition, a complete and reliable biography of Abraham Lincoln.

The great economic depression which began with the stock-market crash in 1929 did not seriously affect Sandburg's personal life or literary plans. Of course a man with the social conscience which all his works display could not be indifferent to the suffering and discouragement of the millions of unemployed or underemployed Americans. Though as a Socialist he had criticized the established economic system, he still believed in the soundness of American society and the ability of its people to make needed changes. To reassert his faith in the common people and to help them regain confidence in themselves, he wrote and published *The People, Yes* (1936). An amalgam of folk wisdom and wit, verbal clichés, tall tales, preaching, slangy conversation, "cracker-barrel" philosophy, and Carl Sandburg cheerfulness, the book served its purpose, as Steinbeck's *Grapes of Wrath* did in another manner. It was wildly praised by people who liked Sandburg, and mostly ignored by those who did not. Mark Van Doren in a lecture on Sandburg at the Library of Congress in 1969 said, "*The People, Yes* is talk, nothing but talk." Van Doren did not mean this in a derogatory sense, and he was right. In this long talky poem we hear the voices of hundreds of Americans, and by listening we learn what kind of people they are, their ambitions, prejudices, superstitions, sense of humor, optimism, generosity, and sense of identity. But *The People, Yes* now seems repetitious and tedious — at least to this reader.

Three years later Sandburg published his truly monumental

Abraham Lincoln: The War Years in four thick volumes, nearly 2500 pages. The critics were enthusiastic, the sales excellent, and it was awarded a Pulitzer Prize in 1940. Sandburg's six volumes of Lincoln biography were a culmination of thirty years of collecting, pondering, and writing about Lincoln. *The War Years* remains his most ambitious work, and it may be his most lasting. In spite of some lapses which scholars have pointed out, it is well documented — factual, solid, meticulously detailed. At times it seems too detailed, as if the author had emptied his filing drawers, but as a consequence Lincoln's life can be seen, felt, and heard from day to day, often in a chaos of conflicting advice, contradictory responsibilities, and demands for decisions which cannot wait for needed information. Under these pressures Lincoln is seen manfully struggling to make the right decisions, and Sandburg does not blink his misjudgments, or sometimes failure to act at all. He is not seen as an idealist, a man of conscience, but always as a shrewd pragmatist, who will save the Union any way he can, with or without slavery. Sandburg also quotes contemporary criticism of Lincoln's failures and imagined failures, so that he may be seen from within and from without. His notorious fondness for stories is copiously illustrated, as might be expected of the author of *The People, Yes.*

Lincoln believed slavery wrong, and he would abolish it if he could, and finally did — or thought he had — but the time must be right. Considering the circumstances so fully presented in *The War Years*, it seems almost miraculous that any man could have held the Union together and won the war in spite of the profusion of graft, incompetent generals and other officials, "Copperhead" subversion, and personal antagonisms within the government, even in the president's Cabinet. That Lincoln did hold on and win makes him seem like a superman, but Sandburg does not load the dice in his favor, as he had at times in *The Prairie Years.* This biography is not only an honest and revealing account of Lincoln's "war years," but also one of the most revealing books ever written on how the American government works — how it looks from the inside in time of great crisis, tragic failures, and creeping success.

Sandburg's enjoyment of his literary triumph was severely tempered by a new, stupendous national crisis which affected him deeply. His total commitment to America's entrance into World War II caused him to undertake the boldest literary experiment of his career, a "novel" covering the whole span of American experience, from the coming of the Pilgrims to the horrors of World War II and the possible consequences of dropping the atom bomb on Japanese cities. This long, complicated work he called *Remembrance Rock* (1948), not from Plymouth Rock, but a rock-shrine in the garden of a fictional Supreme Court justice who slightly resembles Justice Oliver Wendell Holmes. Under the rock the justice had deposited soil from all the places most crucial in American history, and at the end of the novel his grandchildren and their wives and wives-to-be bring the symbolical collection up to date:

"At Remembrance Rock at high noon they laid in metal-bottomed crevices the little prepared copper boxes — gravel from Sicily, sand from Utah Beach on the Normandy coast, rainbow-tinted sand from a coral atoll in the South Pacific, harsh black volcanic ash from Okinawa. They packed in soil at the base of the boulder, leaving no sign of the sacred receptacle underneath."

The whole structure of this novel, if it may be so classified, is as obviously symbolical (its chief fault) as the many kinds of sand under the rock. Some of the characters are historical and some are fictional, representing the earliest white settlers of America, the period of the American Revolution, the migrations into and across the Great Plains, the Civil War, and World War II.

As in all of his writings, Sandburg is facile with conversation in *Remembrance Rock,* but the reader is made too aware of what each speaker "stands for." The story has heroic people and epic action, yet the total effect is that of a patriotic pageant rather than a novel. One can applaud the author's lofty intentions and his great effort without enjoying his art. This literary experiment was a labor of love, and Sandburg was hurt by the failure of the critics to warm up to it. It is not likely to remain as permanently valuable as his one-volume *Abraham Lincoln* (1954), his "distillation" of *The Prairie Years* and *The War Years,* or his big *Complete Poems.*

When the *Complete Poems* appeared in 1950, it was widely reviewed, yet did not receive the high praise of Sandburg's Lincoln biographies. This may have been partly because the fashions in poetry had changed since the years of the depression when *The People, Yes* was so well received. Poetry was now cerebral, dense, and intricately allusive under the influence of Pound and Eliot. The objections to Sandburg's poems were not so much their sententiousness, for Pound and Eliot were as sententious in their own ways as any poet could be, but to his irreverent attitude toward the art of poetry. One of the reviewers of *Complete Poems* was William Carlos Williams, whose poems might appear to be as spontaneously improvised as Sandburg's, but Williams had taken to brooding on his art and concocting theories about how an American poet ought to write, and he thought Sandburg had not given enough thought to these matters. Of course the "New Critics" frowned upon all tendentious poetry, and regarded structure, imagery, tension, and irony as more important than message. They did not so much condemn Sandburg as ignore him, because, they thought, he structured his poems by intuition or whim, and gave these critics few subtleties or ambiguities to challenge their ingenuity. In brief, Sandburg did not need to be explicated.

Complete Poems contains in chronological order the six books of poems (not counting the three privately printed booklets) Sandburg had published before 1950. Its appearance should have given critics an excellent opportunity to evaluate Sandburg's whole career as a poet. But actually none of the reviewers for major publications undertook this task. In fact, their reviews gave the impression that Sandburg was still the "Chicago poet" of 1916, that he had not grown or changed significantly. Evidently it was easier to fall back on the old clichés and stereotypes than to read (or reread) these more than seven hundred poems — seventy-two in a "New Section," some published for the first time anywhere.

Sandburg *had* grown, *had* changed, and several of his finest poems were to be found in the "New Section." Probably the critics had not read the best of these new poems, though they had been published before, but in magazines regarded as nonliterary: "The Fireborn Are at Home in Fire" and "Mr. Longfellow and His Boy" in *Collier's Magazine*; "The Long Shadow of Lincoln: A Litany," in the *Saturday Evening Post*; and the elegy on President Roosevelt, "When Death Came April Twelve 1945," in *Woman's Home Companion*. Of course it is true that one would not expect poems of such high literary quality (or even poems at all) in these mass publications, but a work of art should not be judged by the place of its unveiling.

By 1950 Sandburg had, in the eyes of some critics, two counts against him: he was so famous that he could sell his poems at high prices, and his poems were read and enjoyed by a large public. Even Frost was beginning to suffer from his popularity, but he had several critics of considerable prestige to defend him. Also his life-style protected him to some extent from the curse of success. But Sandburg's folksy manners and his love affair with "the people" were a constant affront and irritant to academic minds, and most literary critics were, and are, either in or close to the academic world. This is not special pleading for Sandburg; it is one observer's explanation of the manner in which *Complete Poems* was reviewed. The fact that the book won the Pulitzer Prize in poetry for that year does not contradict this explanation, nor do the honorary degrees showered upon Sandburg by universities.

In a preface called modestly "Notes for a Preface" Sandburg quotes with approval theories of poetry from Yeats, Synge, Macaulay, and Oliver Wendell Holmes. For example, from Synge: "When men lose their poetic feeling for ordinary life, and cannot write poetry of ordinary things, their exalted poetry is likely to lose its strength of exaltation, in the way men cease to build beautiful churches when they have lost happiness in building shops. Many of the older poets, such as Villon and Herrick and Burns, used the whole of their personal life as their material, and the verse written in this way was read by strong men, and thieves, and deacons, not by little cliques only." It is hardly necessary to add that Sandburg tried to be just such a poet.

In defense of his abandoning rhyme and meter Sandburg quotes a famous rhymester, Dr. Oliver Wendell Holmes: "Rhythm alone is a tether, and not a very long one. But rhymes are iron fetters . . ." Tethers and fetters had always been intolerable to Sandburg, as he discovered as early as 1905. Also as a reader and contributor to *Poetry* in its early years, he was aware of the arguments for and against "free verse," a form (or, as its opponents said, lack of form) in which the phrase is the prosodic unit and the words themselves create their own rhythms. More important than where Sandburg learned free-verse techniques is the fact that he had an excellent ear for the musical sequence of sounds, the balancing and counterpointing of phrase against phrase. Sandburg wrote for both the ear and the eye. His famous "Chicago" poem has an almost architectural structure, beginning with the short, pithy salutation epithets:

> Hog Butcher for the World,
> Tool Maker, Stacker of Wheat . . .

Then come the twelve factual statements modified by the poet's own affirmation blocked out in parallel form:

> They tell me you are wicked and I believe them, for I have seen your painted women under the gas lamps luring the farm boys. . . .

The seventh statement emphasizes the series of participles by spacing them as single lines, or verses:

> Fierce as a dog with tongue lapping for action, cunning as a savage pitted against the wilderness,
> > Bareheaded,
> > Shoveling,
> > Wrecking,
> > Planning,
> > Building, breaking, rebuilding . . .

Both the line breaks and the accents in the phrases play variations on the tempo, slowing or speeding up the sounds to add emphasis. The difference between these long lines and ordinary prose is in the skillful paralleling and accumulating of grammatical units (phrases and clauses). The resulting rhythm is grammatical, or rhetorical, rather than metrical.

Though scarcely any two of Sandburg's poems look alike on the page, or sound alike when read aloud, his sense of form seldom faltered. Notice the pattern of the opening lines of "Pencils" (*Smoke and Steel*):

> > Pencils
> > telling where the wind comes from
> > > open a story.

> > Pencils
> > telling where the wind goes
> > > end a story.

> > > These eager pencils
> > > come to a stop

> . . . only . . . when the stars high over
> come to a stop.

"Canadians and Pottawatomies" (*Good Morning, America*) is almost as syllabic (i.e., equal number of syllables in each line) as a poem by Marianne Moore:

> I have seen a loneliness sit
> in the dark and nothing lit up.
> I have seen a loneliness sit
> in the dark lit up like a Christ-
> mas tree, a Hallowe'en pumpkin.

One of the many ways in which Sandburg's sense of rhythm became more subtle and sensitive was in his handling of syllabic weight, timbre, and vowel tone. This development culminated in the marvelous tone poem "When Death Came April Twelve 1945," which opens:

> Can a bell ring in the heart
> telling the time, telling a moment,
> telling off a stillness come,
> in the afternoon a stillness come
> and now never come morning?

The bell intones throughout the elegy, not mechanically as in Poe's "The Bells," but resonating the deep feelings of the nation grieving for its lost commander, and the sons lost in the South Pacific or on European soil, all now sleeping after toil and battle. The tones of the poem, reinforcing the images of stillness and silence, have the empathy of cleansing and calming the emotions of the readers (hearers). In every technical detail the elegy is almost perfectly ordered, timed, and developed from the opening "Can a bell ring in the heart" to

> the somber consoles rolling sorrow,
> the choirs in ancient laments — chanting:
> > "Dreamer, sleep deep,
> > Toiler, sleep long,

Carl Sandburg

> Fighter, be rested now,
> Commander, sweet good night."

Though Sandburg's patriotism had never been aroused before as it was during World War II, when he was willing to use his talents in any way possible to aid the preservation of a "free world," he was no blind patriot or jingoist. For the poem he read at William and Mary College in 1944, "The Long Shadow of Lincoln: A Litany," he used for an epigraph a quotation from Lincoln's 1862 message to Congress: "We can succeed only by concert. . . . The dogmas of the quiet past are inadequate to the stormy present. The occasion is piled high with difficulty, and we must rise with the occasion. As our case is new so we must think anew and act anew. We must disenthrall ourselves. . . ."

Sandburg knew the importance of *disenthralling ourselves* in the aftermath of World War II. His "Litany" begins:

> Be sad, be cool, be kind,
> remembering those now dreamdust
> hallowed in the ruts and gullies,
> solemn bones under the smooth blue sea,
> faces warblown in a falling rain.

Remember and weep, he says, but "Make your wit a guard and cover." Looking toward peace and the difficulties of maintaining it, " 'We must disenthrall ourselves.' "

> There is dust alive
> with dreams of The Republic,
> with dreams of the Family of Man
> flung wide on a shrinking globe
>
> . . . .
>
> The earth laughs, the sun laughs
> over every wise harvest of man,
> over man looking toward peace
> by the light of the hard old teaching:
> "We must disenthrall ourselves."

Few men were less warped by the war, better kept their wit, or

39

remained as sane as Carl Sandburg. In a group of poems for the
"Present Hour" there is "Jan, the Son of Thomas," who asks:

> Was I not always a laughing man?
> Did I ever fail of ready jests?
> Have I added a final supreme jest?
> They may write where my ashes quiver:
>> "He loved mankind for its very faults.
>> He knew how to forget all wars past.
>>> He so acted
>>> as to forget the next war."

Sandburg did not believe with a certain "handsome mournful
galoot" (T. S. Eliot?) that "The human race is its own Enemy
Number One."

> For him the Family of Man stinks now
>> and if you look back
>> for him it always has stunk.

In "Many Handles" Sandburg warns against "abstractions"
and rigid classifications:

> In the Dark Ages many there and then
> had fun and took love and made visions
> and listened when Voices came.
> Then as now were the Unafraid.
> Then as now, "What if I am dropped into levels
>> of ambiguous dust and covered
>> over and forgotten? Have I in my
>> time taken worse?"

> . . . .

> Should it be the Dark Ages recur, will there be
> again the Immeasurable Men, the Incalculable
> Women?

Though the poem ends with a question, the implication is
plain that there will be great men and women for a new Dark
Age, if it comes. In spite of a terrible premonition of a future
atomic war, Sandburg counsels in "The Unknown War,"

Be calm, collected, easy.
In the face of the next war to come, be calm.
In the faint light and smoke of the flash and the mushroom
  of the first bomb blast of the Third World War, keep
  your wits collected.

. . . .

  We shall do the necessary.
  We shall meet the inevitable.

Thirteen years after the appearance of *Complete Poems*, Sandburg published still another volume of poetry called *Honey and
Salt*. The title poem is skeptical, witty, and philosophical on the
permanence of love.

  Is there any way of measuring love?
  Yes but not till long afterward
  when the beat of your heart has gone
  many miles, far into the big numbers.
Is the key to love in passion, knowledge, affection?
All three — along with moonlight, roses, groceries,
givings and forgivings, gettings and forgettings,
  keepsakes and room rent,
  pearls of memory along with ham and eggs.

If love is "locked away and kept," it "gathers dust and mildew."
How long does it last? "As long as glass bubbles handled with
care / or two hot-house orchids in a blizzard / or one solid im-
movable steel anvil . . ." But

  There are sanctuaries
    holding honey and salt.
  There are those who
    spill and spend.

Many of the poems in this volume are about love, which was
never sweeter or more savory than now for this eighty-five-year-
old lover. Several poems are affectionate devotions to his one and
only wife, and "Out of the Rainbow End" is a fond compliment
to his brother-in-law Edward Steichen, whose hobby was grow-

ing delphiniums. But Sandburg knows also that "Love Is a Deep and a Dark and a Lonely":

> and you take it deep take it dark
> and take it with a lonely winding
> and when the winding gets too lonely
> then may come the windflowers
>
> . . . .
>
> like leaves of windflowers bending low
> and bending to be never broken.

The longest and most ambitious poem in *Honey and Salt* is "Timesweep." The theme might be said to be the same as "Wilderness" (1918), in which the poet lyrically boasted of his kinship with foxes, wolves, and other wild animals. But "Timesweep" is both more genuinely lyrical and more philosophical, lyrical in the poet's empathy with the natural forces and creatures with which he feels a sympathetic kinship, and philosophical in his knowledge of his place in the cosmic scheme. Since Sandburg has so often been compared with Whitman by many critics, it is interesting to place this poem beside passages treating the same theme in "Song of Myself." In section 31 Whitman declares:

> I find I incorporate gneiss, coal, long-threaded moss, fruits,
> grains, esculent roots,
> And am stucco'd with quadrupeds and birds all over,
> And have distanced what is behind me for good reasons,
> But call any thing back again when I desire it.

Then in section 44 Whitman returns to his evolutionary transmigration:

> I am an acme of things accomplish'd, and I an encloser of
> things to be.
>
> My feet strike an apex of the apices of the stairs,
> On every step bunches of ages, and larger bunches between
> the steps,
> All below duly travel'd, and still I mount and mount.
>
> . . . .

Before I was born out of my mother generations guided me,
My embryo has never been torpid, nothing could overlay it.

For it the nebula cohered to an orb,
The long slow strata piled to rest it on,
Vast vegetables gave it sustenance,
Monstrous sauroids transported it in their mouths and deposited it with care.

Sandburg's poem is more personal, less "prophetic" in tone, more aware of human limitations, but the lyrical utterance of a sensitive man who enjoys the sights and sounds of his physical existence:

The pink nipples of the earth in springtime,
The long black eyelashes of summer's look,
The harvest laughter of tawny autumn,
The winter silence of land in snow covers,
Each speaks its own oaths of the cool and the flame
of naked possessions clothed and come naked again:
The sea knows it all.
They all crept out of the sea.

The poet wonders where he came from, and whether there is any going back:

Is it told in my dreams and hankerings, looking
back at what I was, seeing what I am?
Like so a man talking to himself
of the bitter, the sweet, the bittersweet:
he had heard likenings of himself:
Cock of the walk, brave as a lion, fierce as a tiger,
Stubborn as a mule, mean as a louse, crazy as a bedbug,
Soft as a kitten, slimy as an octopus, one poor fish.

Yes, man, "proud man, with a peacock strut" is "a beast out of the jungle," an animal related to all the other animals. Frank Norris and other American naturalists of the late nineteenth century had used this thought to demolish man's pretensions to a special creation in the image of God and his delusions of free will. Sandburg has no such intentions:

43

> What is this load I carry out of yesterday?
> What are these bygones of dreams, moans, shadows?
> What jargons, what gibberish, must I yet unlearn?

He knows that his origins are in a "dim plasm in the sea . . . a drop of jelly," and the countless swimmers and crawlers who preceded the creature called man:

> I have had a thousand fish faces, sea faces,
> sliding off into land faces, monkey faces —
>   I began in a dim green mist
>   of floating faces.

He acknowledges his kindred and feels a degree of identity with them, and wonders what right he has to feel wiser than they. To the elephant he says the "Ignorance we share and share alike is immeasurable."

> I have been woven among meshes of long ropes
> and fine filaments: older than the rocks and
> fresh as the dawn of this morning today are
> the everliving roots who begot me,
> who poured me as one more seeker
> one more swimmer in the gold and gray procession
> of phantoms laughing, fighting, singing, moan-
> ing toward the great cool calm of the fixed
> return to the filaments of dust.

But he also knows that he is "more than a traveler out of Nowhere":

> Sea and land, sky and air, begot me Somewhere.
> Where I go from here and now, or if I go at all again, the
>   Maker of sea and land, of sky and air, can tell.

Knowledge that some almost infinite (or perhaps infinite) chain of life begot him out of Nowhere to Somewhere gives Sandburg sufficient assurance of a *purpose* at work, however humanly unknowable. He will not worry about theology, or teleology. Yet "Timesweep" throws more light on Sandburg's philosophy than any other literary work of his. At the end of this last poem we

44

find a summation of his humanism, rooted in his early socialism, and consolidated by a lifetime of effort to propagate the idea that the Family of Man is One Man:

> There is only one man in the world
> and his name is All men.
>
> . . . .
>
> There is only one Maker in the world
> and His children cover the earth
> and they are named All God's Children.

The poet who wrote this poem had come a long way on the road of art since writing "Chicago." No one knows the range of Sandburg who has not read the "new" poems in his collected *Complete Poems* and observed the further enrichment of his canon in *Honey and Salt*. In his "Notes for a Preface" to *Complete Poems* he remarked: "I have written by different methods and in a wide miscellany of moods and have seldom been afraid to travel in lands and seas where I met fresh scenes and new songs. All my life I have been trying to learn to read, to see and hear, and to write. At sixty-five I began my first novel, and the five years lacking a month I took to finish it, I was still traveling, still a seeker. I should like to think that as I go on writing there will be sentences truly alive, with verbs quivering, with nouns giving color and echoes. It could be, in the grace of God, I shall live to be eighty-nine, as did Hokusai, and speaking my farewell to earthly scenes, I might paraphrase: 'If God had let me live five years longer I should have been a writer.' "

Carl Sandburg did live to be eighty-nine, and he did not need five additional years to become a writer; he had been a writer, a prolific one, and at times a masterful one, for many years. When he became a poet is a subject on which critics have disagreed, and will doubtless continue to do so, but we might paraphrase his quotation from the Japanese painter and say that God created Sandburg a writer, but by his own efforts he became a poet.

⤻ Selected Bibliography

Works of Carl Sandburg

The titles listed below include the published writings of Carl Sandburg with the exception of limited editions, prefaces and introductions to works by other authors, addresses, and recorded readings and talks.

ANTHOLOGIES

Walt Whitman's *Leaves of Grass*, with an introduction by Carl Sandburg. New York: Boni and Liveright, 1921.
The American Songbag. New York: Broadcast Music, 1927.
New American Songbag. New York: Broadcast Music [1950].

BIOGRAPHY AND AUTOBIOGRAPHY

Abraham Lincoln: The Prairie Years. 2 vols. New York: Harcourt, Brace, 1926.
Abe Lincoln Grows Up, with illustrations by James Daugherty. New York: Harcourt, Brace [1928]. (From *Abraham Lincoln: The Prairie Years.*)
Steichen the Photographer. New York: Harcourt, Brace, 1929.
Mary Lincoln: Wife and Widow (with Paul M. Angle). New York: Harcourt, Brace, 1932.
Abraham Lincoln: The War Years. 4 vols. New York: Harcourt, Brace, 1939.
Storm over the Land. New York: Harcourt, Brace, 1942. (From *Abraham Lincoln: The War Years.*)
Always the Young Strangers. New York: Harcourt, Brace, 1953.
Abraham Lincoln: The Prairie Years and the War Years. New York: Harcourt, Brace, 1954. ("A distillation.")

FOR YOUNG READERS

Rootabaga Stories. New York: Harcourt, Brace, 1922.
Rootabaga Pigeons. New York: Harcourt, Brace, 1923.
Abe Lincoln Grows Up. New York: Harcourt, Brace, 1928.
Early Moon. New York: Harcourt, Brace, 1930.
Prairie-Town Boy. New York: Harcourt, Brace, 1955. (From *Always the Young Strangers.*)

46

Wind Song. New York: Harcourt, Brace, 1960.
The Wedding Procession of the Rag Doll and the Broom Handle and Who Was in It. New York: Harcourt, Brace, 1967.

NOVEL AND STORIES

Potato Face. New York: Harcourt, Brace, 1930. ("Rootabaga stories for adults.")
Remembrance Rock. New York: Harcourt, Brace, 1948.

POETRY

In Reckless Ecstasy. Galesburg: Asgard Press, 1904. (Private press.)
The Plaint of a Rose. Galesburg: Asgard Press [1905?].
Incidentals. Galesburg: Asgard Press [1905].
Chicago Poems. New York: Henry Holt, 1916.
Cornhuskers. New York: Henry Holt, 1918.
Smoke and Steel. New York: Harcourt, Brace, 1920.
Slabs of the Sunburnt West. New York: Harcourt, Brace, 1922.
Good Morning, America. New York: Harcourt, Brace, 1928.
The People, Yes. New York: Harcourt, Brace, 1936.
Complete Poems. New York: Harcourt, Brace, 1950.
Honey and Salt. New York: Harcourt, Brace, 1963.

SELECTED EDITIONS OF POETRY

Selected Poems of Carl Sandburg, edited by Rebecca West. New York: Harcourt, Brace, 1926.
Poems of the Midwest. Cleveland and New York: World Publishing Company, 1946. (*Chicago Poems* and *Cornhuskers.*)
The Sandburg Range. New York: Harcourt, Brace, 1957. (Selection of poetry and prose.)
Harvest Poems: 1910–1960. New York: Harcourt, Brace, 1960.

PROSE MISCELLANY

The Chicago Race Riots (July 1919), with an introduction by Walter Lippmann. New York: Harcourt, Brace and Howe, 1919. (Reprinted from the *Chicago Daily News.*)
Home Front Memo. New York: Harcourt, Brace, 1943.
The Photographs of Abraham Lincoln (with Frederick H. Meserve). New York: Harcourt, Brace, 1944.
Lincoln Collector: The Story of Oliver R. Barrett's Great Private Collection. New York: Harcourt, Brace, 1949.

Address before a Joint Session of Congress, February 12, 1959. New York: Harcourt, Brace [1959]. (Published also in Washington, D.C., Worcester, Mass., and Cedar Rapids, Iowa.)

LETTERS

The Letters of Carl Sandburg, edited by Herbert Mitgang. New York: Harcourt, Brace and World, 1968. (Contains a useful chronological table.)

Bibliographies

Harry Golden's *Carl Sandburg* (see Biographies below) has a checklist of Sandburg's works and *Honey and Salt* (see Poetry above) has a classified checklist.

The Sandburg Range: An Exhibit of Materials from Carl Sandburg's Library Placed on Display in the University of Illinois Library on January 6, 1958, with an introduction by John T. Flanagan; bibliographical descriptions and notes by Leslie W. Dunlap. University of Illinois Library, Adah Patton Memorial Fund, Publication Number Six. [Urbana, 1958.]

Van Doren, Mark. *Carl Sandburg,* with a bibliography of Sandburg materials in the collections of the Library of Congress. Washington, D.C.: Library of Congress, 1969. (This is the most extensive bibliography of Sandburg, including translations, addresses, introductions and prefaces, articles, interviews and conversations, manuscripts, musical settings, phonograph records, motion pictures.)

Biographies

Callahan, North. *Carl Sandburg: Lincoln of Our Time.* New York: New York University Press, 1970.

Golden, Harry. *Carl Sandburg.* Cleveland and New York: World Publishing Company, 1961.

Critical Studies

Allen, Gay Wilson. "Carl Sandburg: Fire and Smoke," *South Atlantic Quarterly,* 59:315–31 (Summer 1960).

Basler, Roy P. "Your Friend the Poet — Carl Sandburg," *Midway,* 10:3–15 (Autumn 1969).

Cargill, Oscar. "Carl Sandburg: Crusader and Mystic," *College English,* 11:365–72 (April 1950).

Van Doren, Mark. *Carl Sandburg.* Washington, D.C.: Library of Congress, 1969.

Williams, William Carlos. Review of Carl Sandburg's *Complete Poems,* in *Poetry,* 7–8:345ff (September 1951).